# HOW TO SAVE LIVES THROUGH MARKETING

### "THE 10 MARKETING SECRETS TO ATTRACT NEW PATIENTS WITH LITTLE TO NO MONEY"

## "BE A MARKETING SUPER HERO"

# How to Save Lives through Marketing

## The 10 marketing strategies that will help you change your community and change the world

*By Dr John Bergman*

# Table of Contents

### *How to Save Lives through Marketing*

*The 10 marketing strategies that will help you change your community and change the world*

I am a subluxation based corrective Chiropractor and I've been in practice for 15 years. I have about 800 patient visits a week and over 95% of my patients pay in cash (I don't like insurance). I have an awesome team – we train on office procedures and patient interaction 3 days a week, and we are a Monday-to-Thursday office so we have regular 3-day weekends. Yes! This is a dream practice!

The greatest joy I have is making a difference in people's lives. We change our patients' perception of their potential – by reversing Arthritis, correcting High Blood Pressure, eliminating Fibromyalgia, etc., always using drug-free solutions. We just use the power that *made* the body in the first place to then *heal* the body.

It wasn't always like this. When I started in practice, I was working in a multi-doctor practice and it was commission only. I started at three office visits per week, and those visits were from my mom – Monday, Wednesday and Friday. As you can imagine, it took me a while to save up for a cup of

Starbucks. The clinic didn't provide me with any patients until I made it to at least four months in practice – a sink or swim proposition.

I was also teaching part time at Cleveland Chiropractic L.A., which put food on the table but not much more. I had two sons, age 5 and 11, and we were staying in a 10' x 12' room in a 30-year-old mobile home. My school, Cleveland Chiropractic College, had given me one of the finest educations in the world. I knew anatomy, physiology, neurology, microbiology, biochemistry, multiple Chiropractic techniques, and I was skilled in diagnostics and pathologies. In short, I was one of the finest trained doctors on the planet. However, school had taught me absolutely *no* business skills. I had all this passion and all these skills and absolutely no idea how to get patients.

I did have a business background, however, and I had been self-employed for nine years before I entered Chiropractic College. And every business that I started, I did it with very little capital – lots of enthusiasm but very little cash. As a brand new Chiropractor, I knew it would take me some time to build up the practice of my dreams, but with kids and bills I had to get it going fast. With only a vision of my dream practice and absolutely no idea how to get there, I was in panic mode.

Let me tell you: reality hits hard. Like Rocky Balboa said: "Nobody is going to hit as hard as life." So there's that twisting-of-your-gut feeling that you get when your kids want something and you just can't get it for them, or when you're putting the bills in those three piles: 1. Gotta pay; 2. Gotta pay now, really; 3. Gotta pay because they're past due. To keep a positive mental outlook with my patients and my family – and with myself – was hard when all I could do was feed the kids and pay pile #3.

There is a story that a lot of motivational speakers have used about how the early settlers came to this country ill prepared. The way the story goes is that the colonists were attacked by the natives and the colonists were losing. During the attack the leaders of the colony rowed out to the boats in the bay. The boats were the only means of escape the colonists had, and the leaders of the colony burned the boats, eliminating the option of escaping. That way there was nothing the settlers could do except be successful or die; there was no escape. My predicament was similar: make it as a Chiropractor or die; there was no plan "B" in my world. Essentially I had burned my boats in the bay. I had no savings, two young kids, a mountain of student loans, and a passion for helping people.

Desperate for a plan to get my practice up and running, I asked every successful Chiropractor what they had done when they started out. I also asked what they read, what they did for motivation . . . I asked them everything. What was amazing was that they all told me what they had done. What was even more amazing was that when I did it, it worked!  So now it is my turn to share it with you….

When I say I had no other option other than success or death, I have to tell you how I came to be a Chiropractor. I was launched into chiropractic by a devastating accident that nearly ended my life. At 30 years old, I was a hard-working single dad when I was hit by a speeding car that left me with two fractured legs, a fractured skull and chest, and a bruised liver and heart. Thankfully, I received the finest medical care and it saved my life. However, after four knee surgeries and multiple medications, I realized that surgeries and drugs were not the answer to regaining health. Disillusioned by the modern symptom-based, mechanistic health care system, I began a quest to find a vitalistic-based healthcare model to help me regain my health.

So the medical world really wasn't offering me hope but at the same time, I was seeing a Chiropractor, and it was interesting, because he was doing adjustments on me while I was in a wheelchair. I don't know if you know this, but if you've ever had two broken legs at one time, you're not mobile. So I'm in the wheelchair, and I'm going in there, and after every operation I'm back in the wheelchair; and wheelchairs are not fun or comfortable. The Chiropractor is adjusting me, and he's saying, "Your body is designed to heal; it's designed to be healthy. Your body can regenerate."

And I said, "No, because I fractured my bones." And he said, "It doesn't matter. Within four or five weeks, your bones are brand new." And I said, "Yeah, but they're operating on my cartilage, my knees, my meniscus." And he said, "Your meniscus can re-grow; it's alive."

And I'm thinking, "Everything this Chiropractor says makes sense and seems to be true." And so at that time I was starting to not believe the medical doctors and their outcome predictions because it was a belief system; it wasn't science. The bleak future health care professionals were predicting for me was based on their beliefs; and they believed that what they said was true. If I had adopted their belief system, I would have a very poor quality of life today.

If I had believed that my body was broken beyond its ability to regenerate, or if I had been sucked into that belief system, my kids would have lost their dad. Thank God I came to the realization that the body is a *self-healing, self-regenerating machine.* And I truly found out that the surgeons, God bless them for their surgical skills, but they were wrong when it came to their perception of health and of human potential. Their perception was wrong. They believed that more surgeries were appropriate and that medications were appropriate.

Disillusioned by the modern symptom-based, mechanistic health care system, I began a quest to find a vitalistic (life) based healthcare model that would help me regain my health. I became a Chiropractor and instructor at Cleveland Chiropractic College in Los Angeles, specializing in Human Dissection Anatomy, Physiology, Biomechanics and multiple Chiropractic techniques. Cleveland Chiropractic College gave me one of the finest educations in the world. I learned about anatomy, physiology, neurology, microbiology and biochemistry. I became skilled in diagnostics and skilled in pathologies, and I became one of the finest trained Doctors on the planet

What I didn't realize at the time I was in school teaching was that I was also learning to rehab my body, and that those techniques would translate into ways to save lives. Having the awareness that people were suffering from dis-eases and discomfort drove me crazy – because I had suffered from what the medical doctors said I would have to suffer from the rest of my life and I had recovered!

I want you to understand that the key to saving lives is knowing that the same power that *made* the body *heals* the body. You as a Chiropractor have the key, and this translates into *a moral and ethical obligation to market to everyone!* Look at the ads on television – 46% are for drugs!

Your community needs you! Look at the following stats regarding chronic disease:

- Chronic diseases kill more than 1.7 million Americans a year.

- Chronic disease is responsible for 7 of 10 deaths in the US.

- 133 million Americans, or 45% of the population, have at least one chronic condition.

- 78 million Americans, or 26% of the population, have multiple chronic conditions.

- In the last 20 years, there has been a 300% increase in childhood obesity in the US.

- In the last 40 years, there has been a 400% increase in childhood chronic diseases in the US.

And the supposed solution to all this has turned into a drug epidemic: the US represents 5% of the world's population and uses 50% of the drugs available on the planet. This problem of chronic disease will soon affect nearly every man, woman, and child, in the US – and drugs are not the answer.

This is how marketing can save lives and it is vital that you understand this fact. Every person on the planet deserves optimal health, but the current disease care system is broken! People are suffering and dying needlessly because the standard of care is to try to drug the symptoms away. Basically, the medical system is making people comfortable while they die early!

So I'll say it again . . . with your education and training as Chiropractors, *you have a moral and ethical obligation to save lives and stop this carnage.* Only through making the general public aware of the fantastic opportunity you are giving them will they preserve their health. You have to take advantage of every opportunity to educate people – and change their belief system – regarding health. If you don't reach people through marketing, your community and the entire planet will suffer.

It may seem that I'm being dramatic, but from my perspective of having been in chronic pain for years and seeing what the standard sick care system was offering me for a solution, it was totally unacceptable. Also, having spent 15 years in Chiropractic, I have seen thousands of patients recover from "incurable" diseases, that is, "incurable if they are treated with patentable chemicals (medications), I can assure you I'm *not* being dramatic.

After my accident, I was told I would be in pain *my whole life*. Think of the loss and the painful future those doctors were predicting for me. I wouldn't be the dad I had hoped to be, so my pain was going to affect my kids as well. I wouldn't be able to play baseball or bike ride or run with my kids. The bleak future health care professionals were predicting for me was based on their belief system and they actually believed that what they said was true. If I had taken on their belief system, I would have had an extremely poor quality of life. If I had believed my body was broken beyond its ability to regenerate, or if I had been sucked into that negative belief system, my kids would basically have lost their dad. Thank God I came to the realization that the body is a *self-healing, self-regenerating machine.*

Today's medical system is reminiscent of the time when the greatest minds on the planet knew without a doubt that the world was *flat* – and they could prove it! In fact, if you disagreed with the Flat Earth belief system, you would have been shunned at the very least or even killed as a dissident.

The medical system of today is broken. According to the Journal of the American Medical Association, approximately, "106,000 people die each year in U.S. Hospitals from properly prescribed drugs." (Those are drugs prescribed at the right time, for the right diagnosis, at the right dosage). Over 2 million suffer serious side effects."(JAMA, 1998). And nearly 50% of our population is going to get diabetes and/or cancer. This is a sick care system that pays doctors for procedures, not for outcomes. "The operation was successful but the patient died" is an old joke, but there is some truth in that old bad joke. The doctors of today are paid for tests and interventions; they are not paid for prevention of disease and optimal health. As Bill Maher once stated: "There is no money in healthy people and there is no money in dead people. The money is in the middle – people who are alive sort of but with one or more chronic conditions…."

The medical system is divided into specialties like gastroenterology, neurology, nephrology, pulmonology, psychiatry, cardiology, etc. Take, for example, a patient with high cholesterol; when he sees the cardiologist he will most likely be prescribed a statin to reduce his cholesterol (even though 75% of all cardiovascular events occur in patients with normal to low cholesterol levels). This commonly used drug causes cholesterol levels to fall, depleting the cholesterol needed for the raw materials for the adrenal glands. The adrenal glands are like the pharmacy of the body, and that complex molecule called cholesterol is the precursor to testosterone, estrogen, adrenalin – virtually everything the adrenals make is from cholesterol. The statins causes a drop in cholesterol, which can lead to depression, which can lead to a visit to the psychiatrist and another prescription, this time an SSRI (Selective Seratonin Reuptake Inhibitor) like Depakot, Prozac, Wellbutrin, etc.

However, if you look up the mechanism of action for SSRIs, you'll find out that it doesn't necessarily slow the uptake of serotonin, and the fact is that the mechanism of action of these SSRI's is "unknown." However, we do know that the side effects can include suicide and suicidal thoughts. This is called medical care? We know that 90% of your body's serotonin is produced by the gut. So could depression really be a gut issue? After seeing thousands of patients who were suffering from Fibromyalgia, anxiety, depression, etc., I can assure you that the solution, and I mean complete recovery for all of these conditions, depends on healthy nerve function and healthy gut function.

The scenario described above is played out millions of times across America. I commonly get patients taking a dozen prescriptions; the record holder for the patient with the most prescriptions is currently at 32! That is 32 different prescriptions taken every day! That is *Flat Earth Thinking*. People are suffering and dying from this broken care system. Right now there are limitless opportunities for doctors who focus on health rather than disease, and who focus on using the body's natural abilities to heal rather than trying to drug the symptoms. As a Chiropractor, with your knowledge and awareness that the body is self-regulating and self-healing, *you have an ethical and moral obligation to save lives*. The tools in this book will help you be part of that revolution in health care. Change the world and save lives!!

# How to use this book and the ten steps listed below:

Read them all the way through first; then go back and start with Step #1. You have to start with the Mind Storming. This will give you a clue as to the *passions* that drive you. You may have an inspiration regarding working with sports teams or working with new moms, or whatever. The only thing that matters is that you are driven by your *passion*.

All of the steps work in every community, and every community is literally *dying* from lack of knowledge, but you have that knowledge. The tools that you possess are ways to let every man, woman and child know that there is another choice for health care. You will be able to provide your clients with a new and brighter future. And *now* is the time to get started.

**Here are the 10 Marketing Secrets that will save lives and change your community and change the world:**

Step #1 – Mind Storming: Some people believe that all the answers of the universe are in your mind. Mind storming is how to access them. I have taught this to dozens of Chiropractors, although not all of them have utilized this powerful technique. It was taught to me by a phenomenally successful Chiropractor – I did it and it **WORKS**!! But you have to **DO** it!! When I first did it, I was in a diner waiting for a court appearance where I was going for custody of my son. So I was not very happy, in fact I was stressed out – but it still worked! Here it is:

(1) Sit down with just you a piece of paper and a pencil. At the top of the paper, write something specific that you want. I wrote "New Patients" because I knew that new patients meant I could make a difference in their lives, in my family, in my finances, and in my community. New Patients meant

everything. Note: make sure that what you write on the top of the page is specific. For example, "happiness," "joy," more money" are too abstract and not focused enough for this process.

(2) Write 20 specific actions you will do to achieve your goal. Everyone can write down 4 or 5 actions; but by thinking and writing down 10, then 15, then 20, you are tapping into a universal intelligence. When I was doing this for the first time, I came up with "Charity Day" and my practice took off like a rocket. If you write "pass out business cards," write a specific number of cards per day. If you write "join an organization," instead, write "join Elks Club" or "join Toastmasters." Be specific in your actions that you write.

This writing of your actions is not a project done over time; you have to start and finish it in one setting. This action is the key to tap into the universal intelligence and tap into your passions. I can't stress enough how important it is to complete this step. This is your marketing map. What you might find is that when you get to actions 10-15 or 15-20, you may have a brilliant insight and want to start that one first. Then go ahead and start there. You don't need to do the actions you have written in the order you have written them. I guarantee you that when you have completed all 20 actions, you will have whatever you wrote on the top of the paper to start with. You have the answers, and Mind

Storming will give you the right direction and stimulate your passion.

**Step #2 – Charity Day:** Call your Chamber of Commerce and get a list of charities in your area. Pick some charities that you want to support, like the Arthritis foundation, church groups, etc., and then call the groups you want to support and ask them if they accept private donations. If they say "Yes," here is the script:

*"I am Dr._____ and as a gift to my community, I feature a charity a few times a year. This year, I would like to feature your organization. For a $20 dollar donation directly to your organization, I will give the individual a 5-point health check-up, including an exam, X-rays if necessary, a report of findings, and even an adjustment. All that is a $275 value for just a $20 donation to your organization. I can take a maximum of 50 people, so that would be a $1,000.00 check to you. Do you have a newsletter in which you can advertise this event?"* (If the answer is yes, find out the month the newsletter comes out and schedule for that month.)

By doing a Charity Day, you get free advertising; you get to help people; and you help an organization that you want to support. Also, introduce yourself to the leaders of the group you are supporting; bring them flyers for the Charity Day; and invite them to your office for a no-charge exam / health check-up. I would recommend doing one charity day a month until you get to capacity; then do one a quarter. I did one a month for one year, then one a quarter for about five years. Now I support charities with my time and cash.

**Step #3 – Weekly Health Classes:** That's right; I said "weekly" and I would recommend Tuesday night from 7:00pm to 7:45pm. This is a lot of work but it will establish you as an expert. And you *must* film them and watch them. Watching yourself is hard because you will see various mistakes in your interactions; but the effort you put into this is vital. Remember, it's not about *you*. People are literally *dying* for the lack of information you have in your head. You owe it to your community and our planet to educate and save lives. Use your passion in every talk and you will make a difference. I have had patients come from around the world as a result of watching my Health videos. Then put your videos on www.youtube.com . You must link the videos to your website as well.

To pick the subjects for your talks, ask your patients, and look at the latest topic on the news. The most popular subjects I have found are: How to Achieve Deep Sleep; Depression Cause and Cure; Brain Health – How to Prevent

Dementia; Arthritis Cause and Cure; Autoimmune Disease Cause and Cure; High Blood Pressure – the Natural Solution; Foot Health; Cure for the Common Cold. There are limitless subjects; just make sure you are *passionate* about what you are speaking about.

The talks must have a beginning, middle, end, and a call to action. Here are some examples of what to include in the Beginning, Middle, and End:

Beginning: You must start with thanking the people for taking time out of their day to get this information; and acknowledge them –they are the leaders that will change the world. Then "begin with the end in mind." Tell them what you will be covering during the talk and that you will have an opportunity for them at the end of your talk that will make a difference in their lives. Then this next part is the most important part of your presentation: ***share some of your story***. Share something about ***yourself*** – your pain, your dreams, your passions; speak from the heart. This will connect you with your audience.

Middle: Bring up current medical approaches (which we know have disastrous effects). Bring up case studies of people that you know have had this condition and that have recovered by using your methods. Bring up science articles and facts to support your position. Great web sites for information are: www.mercola.com, www.whale.to, www.naturalnews.com, www.vaccinationcouncil.org, www.vaclib.org. These are just a few of my favorite sites; you will find many more during your research for your talks.

**End:** Describe the solution in detail, emphasizing how the body heals itself. Make sure you cover all aspects of healing, like healthy nerve supply, good nutrition, exercise, deep sleep, prayer and meditation.

**Call to action:** "Knowing what we do, we as a community have an obligation to save lives. I am offering a 5-point health check-up, usually $275, but tonight only $20; and I'm sure you know some family members and friends who will also benefit from this life-saving offer. I will extend this to them as well. You can sign up yourself for this health check-up and your family members as well; schedule with (Lori) right away." Then ask for any questions.

**Notes**: Have at least one assistant for every 20 people in attendance. Advertise your talks on www.meetup.com, www.facebook.com, www.twitter.com, and have an Upcoming Event board in your office. Make your patients aware of your upcoming talk during your table talk or during your adjustment. Table talk is the 1 minute script you say to your patient during your adjustment so bring up one of three things: 1. Talk about your upcoming talk or event; 2. Mention something about their case; 3. Talk about a health event in the news like the flu shot scam or some type of drug recall.

These weekly classes establish you as the health expert. They will also generate excitement for your clinic and your patients will become raving fans. You will be training your patients to become part of your health revolution team. They will become health experts with what you have taught them and they will make a difference in your community and the world. This will massively increases your new patient referrals because it gives your patients that attend these lectures solid facts and the confidence to approach others with health solutions. This will save more lives and change your community.

# *Co-promote with other businesses. Look to yoga studios, private gyms, etc. Steps #4, 5 and 6 below are examples.*

**Step #4 – Barber Shops or Salons:** get your hair trimmed or shampooed two times a week. Now this seems like a lot, but every hair stylist needs the carpal tunnel rap – here is the script:

"Carpal tunnel syndrome retires Chiropractors and retires hair stylists. Did you know it is a *double crush injury* and *not* a repetitive motion injury? What I mean is, it begins with a pinched nerve in the neck and leads to a muscle imbalance of the forearm. The normal strength ratio of the forearm is 5 to 4; in other words, the flexors are slightly stronger then the extensors (at this point, show the muscles on the back of the arm and show the muscles on the front of the arm). A lot of people squeeze a ball but that is the *wrong* exercise. You need a carpal tunnel exerciser – and I have one here (give them a #32 rubber band and demonstrate the extension exercise for the fingers)."

Also ask to leave your flyers and set up a cross promotion with them – you will send your patients to them and they will send their clients to you. Do this with at least three hair salons.

**Flyers:** Make sure your flyers have a sensational front cover with "fear and solution." Example: "Protect your Family! Over 16,500 deaths per year from over-the-counter pain relievers!! Here is the drug-free solution!" Include a short paragraph about yourself, share a real part of you about what drives you, don't be afraid to reveal a past pain or challenge. People like stories and will identify challenges they have had with the challenges you share, getting them to connect with you. You can also include a case study. Then offer a discount: "Health Checkup" or "Disease Risk Checkup" or "Pain Solution Checkup." Try different themes on your flyers and change them about once a month to see what works. Get creative; be bold; lives literally depend on this information getting out there.

For more great marketing tips scan the QR code below or go to http://0s4.com/r/YCUADN

**Step #5 – Partner with Community Businesses:** For example, get your dry cleaning done at two or more different dry cleaners and ask to leave your flyers. Set up a cross-promotion with them where you will refer your patients to them and they will refer their clients to you. Other examples of cross promotions: yoga studios (also great for health talks), private gyms, workout studios, dance studios, colonic clinics, health food stores, etc. When you approach the owners, make an offer for a no-charge checkup and/or a tour of your clinic. They are in business and all businesses require exposure. Have each business you choose to cross-promote with, make special coupons so you can promote your clients to them and you will make special coupons to promote their clients to you.

**Step #6 – Join a Church Group, Rotary Club, Chamber of Commerce, Toastmasters – just join something!** and get involved in your community to help out. Offer to do a Charity Day to generate money for any group you belong to. This will get you well known and you will develop a reputation for community service and trust. Any group that you join or support has people in it that will die early without your care. Each group you join will present opportunities for speaking engagements or Charity Days. Any community group that you support will cause more people to be aware of you; and good energy out causes good energy to flow back to you. How many people need to be checked for subluxations? EVERYONE! That means you have a duty to let everyone know that there is an alternative to the sick care system and You Are The Solution!!!

**Step #7 – Blog Talk Radio:** This is a free service that the general public and your patients have access to. It only takes half an hour with about one hour of prep. This is a vital part of creating a reputation as a health care expert, and this will separate you from every other Chiropractor on the planet. Make sure you post your radio show on iTunes so the public can have access to it. The radio show only requires a land line and a computer, and it looks great on a resume for future speaking engagements. The mindset for the radio show is to convey the simplest information that you have. For example, "93% of all headaches come from the neck" or "NSAID's like Advil®, Ibuprofen®, Aleve®, etc. inhibit proteoglygan production and that is the building block of *cartilage*." So just by suggesting water or Omega-3's, you can save lives.

I would recommend you do the radio show on the same subject as your weekly Health Talk. Mention that you have a weekly radio show and a weekly health education class that is video recorded to every group you join and every business you cross promote with. Advertise your radio show on Facebook, Twitter, and an event board in your office. The radio show further establishes you as the health expert. You will be changing the public's perception of a Chiropractor as back pain doctor to the role Chiropractors need to assume as the true health solution doctors!!

*"The doctor of the future will give no medicine, but will interest her or his patients in the care of the human frame, in a proper diet, and in the cause and prevention of disease."* Thomas A. Edison

Chiropractors are the Doctors of the future here today!!

**Step #8 –Table Talk:** Take advantage of the time with your patients. Do NOT talk about sports or current events. When you are adjusting patients, talk about one of three different subjects: 1. Something about their case (exercise, re-exam coming up, more flexibility, compliment on better water drinking or exercise compliance, etc.); 2. An upcoming event, like a charity day or this month's special at your clinic, the subject of your health talk or your radio show, etc.; 3. A current health event. Read at least two newsletters a day, particularly those recommended below….

http://hsionline.com/hsi-e-alert-sign-up-today/ This is the Health Science Institute. Jenny Thompson writes this and it is cutting edge. Or read www.mercola.com or www.naturalnews.com. These newsletters will keep you informed and up to date, and you will get a reputation for being a health authority. The information will also give you material for your radio show.

**Step #9 – Focused Health Screening:** Of course I do not mean Spinal Screenings – the people at these events or places are stuck in a sick care system; and they likely are not aware that a true disease reversal system exists. Some are so stuck in the matrix of sick care that they won't want to get out. (Yes, I know that is a play on a quote from the movie *The Matrix* but it's absolutely true.

Also, develop "elevator speeches." An elevator speech is a 10-15 second sound bite to capture people's attention. Here are a few examples:

- " Did you know that 93% of all headaches come from the neck, and I (Chiropractors) fix the neck, thus fixing the source of the headaches."

- "If the current vaccination schedule doesn't change by 2026, that is the year that the number of kids with autism will outnumber the kids without autism."

- "Carpal tunnel syndrome and shoulder problems come from the neck; I fix the neck, the source of those symptoms."

- "Asthma is not a problem of the lungs but a smooth muscle problem of the lungs, and the nerves control those muscles, so asthma is a nerve supply problem. I fix the source of the asthma."

- "Antidepressant drugs have the side effect of suicide. They are supposed to help with serotonin in the brain, but 90% of your body's serotonin is produced in the gut. I fix the gut and that solves the source of depression."

When communicating at health talks and with others, start using the term "I" instead of "Chiropractic". The goal is to promote *you* and by building your reputation you will also be changing the publics' perception of Chiropractors and the first choice in health care.

The body is self regulating and self healing. All we as Chiropractors do is remove the impingements to healing and educate our patients on ways to get their optimal health back. I always tell my patients: "I move the bone and God does the healing." or "I am a wrench in the hands of God." The truth is, the power that *made* the body is the only power that can *heal* the body. This sounds like old-school Chiropractic philosophy; however, it is more based on science than modern medicine is. We now know the human body is more energy than matter from a quantum physics level and we are working with the power that controls and coordinates the body. Our Chiropractic approach is more based on science than prescribing medications that either poison an enzyme or block a receptor site. The drug approach is not based on health or science.

Here is a great quote from B.J. Palmer: "We Chiropractors work with the subtle substance of the soul. We release the imprisoned impulses, a tiny rivulet of force, that emanates from the mind and flows over the nerves to the cells and stirs them to life. We deal with the magic power that transforms common food into living, loving, thinking clay; that robes the earth with beauty, and hues and scents the flowers with the glory of the air."

**Focused Health Screening Events:**

**For running events:** Have a bench and offer a quick check to prevent shin splints. Check for patellar tracking and check for proper foot biomechanics. I demonstrate this on YouTube:

http://0s4.com/r/TKL48Y

This will give you a tool to make people aware that you are a biomechanical expert, while most people at running events are concerned with performance and injury prevention. Also have a few blocks of wood, like 8-inch blocks from a 4"X4," and have folks stretch the calves. This will make your booth very popular. You then have an obligation to give them an opportunity to get a health check at your clinic.

**For standard events:** Look at people walking by and I mean *look*. You will see *forward head carriage* that will clue you into all of the symptoms associated with forward head carriage, like: headaches, allergies, high blood pressure, altered thyroid function, rotator cuff injuries, attention deficit disorder, carpal tunnel syndrome, etc. Be bold; tell the people walking by about the condition they have without them telling you they have it. You will be amazed at how accurate you will be in your predictions. Be bold; use your elevator speeches for pattern interrupts. Remember lives depend on your connecting with those who need you. Every parent that has a child needs to know about the dangers of vaccinations. Every person with forward head carriage needs to know that this is a source of arm symptoms and/or High Blood Pressure. The screening events are not about you; lives are depending on your connecting. The knowledge you have comes with a responsibility to share it.

Have on hand at least four card stock handouts with solutions for Headaches, Fibromyalgia, Carpal Tunnel Syndrome, and Attention Deficit Disorder. Make sure the handouts have some short facts about a condition the person is interested in and on the back contact info for you. Here are some examples for the screening handout solutions:

---

## Headache Source and Solution <u>Know the Facts!!!</u>

- 93% of Headaches Begin in the Neck

- Medications for Headaches have disastrous effects on the body

- The most common Drugs used for Headaches cause destruction of cartilage

- Medications for Headaches do nothing for the cause of Headaches

- Chiropractic care goes after the source!

Get the source checked:

Your Name and # Here

Headache Solution Expert

---

---

## Fibromyalgia Solutions Know the Facts!!!

**- The Source is from the fight or flight nervous system (we fix the cause)**

**- Medications do nothing for the cause of FMS**

**- The medical world thinks FMS is incurable (it is curable but not with drugs)**

**- Health is the Natural state of the body!!**

**- Chiropractic care goes after the source!**

Get the source checked:

Your Name and # Here

Fibromyalgia Solution Expert

---

## Attention Deficit Disorder Drug Free Solution

### Know the Facts!!!

- The Source is from the fight or flight nervous system (we fix the cause)

- Medications do nothing for the cause of ADD and ADHD

- ADD and ADHD are from food deficiencies or toxicities!!!

- Healthy Body equals Healthy Brain Function!

- Expect Fast Results!!!

Get the source checked:

Your Name and # Here

ADD and ADHD Solution Expert

Take standard 8.5"x11" card stock and divide it into thirds width-wise so you end up with three pieces approx. 8.5 x 3.5 inches. On one side put directions for an exercise for, or solution to, Headaches, Fibromyalgia, Carpal Tunnel Syndrome, and Attention Deficit Disorder. On the back of the card, put your offer and a map to your clinic, a link to your web site, and a QR code to a video of you demonstrating an appropriate exercise or a testimonial from a patient or patients who have recovered from that condition.

If you are just starting out and you don't have testimonials yet, have a video of yourself explaining your drug-free, solution-oriented approach.

Here is an example of my favorite card handout for screening events:

The solution for CTS (Carpal Tunnel Syndrome): Have a pile of #32 rubber bands handy so you can give out "free Carpal Tunnel Syndrome exercises" and an explanation that Carpal Tunnel Syndrome is a double crush injury, meaning it begins in the neck. So they have to get their neck checked. For a great handout at screening events, get some bright card stock and make the flier 8.5" X 5.5" so you get 2 handouts per page. Cut a small slit in one corner of the card and put a #32 rubber band in it. Add some cool facts about Carpal Tunnel Syndrome like:

---

## Carpal Tunnel Exerciser
/ /

### Know the Facts!!!                    (cut a double slit
here and place rubber band here)

- **Double Crush Injury (begins in the Neck)**

- **Surgery is 80% non-effective (missing the source)**

- **Wrist braces make the muscle imbalance worse**

- **Medication treatment has disastrous results**

- **Chiropractic care goes after the source!**

Get the source checked:

(Your Name and Number here)

Carpal Tunnel Syndrome Expert

---

This is the free Carpal Tunnel exerciser. On the back of the card stock, put your offer and a map to your clinic, a link to your web site, and a QR code to a video of you demonstrating this exercise.

Having free gifts makes health screenings fun! I demonstrate this on my video at:

http://0s4.com/r/A09N6Z

**Step #10 – Your Marketing Mindset:** During any personal interaction, having the correct mindset is vital. This is why you want to tell your staff to *smile* when they answer the phone because people will *"hear the smile."* A positive mental attitude will come through in their conversation. So just like training for a sports event, you have to train to have the right outcome for any personal interaction.

# The Quality of your Life is dependent on the Quality of your Communication!!

There are two types of communication: Type 1 – Communication with Others; Type 2 – Communication with Yourself.

**Type 1: When you are communicating with others, the words you choose are just a small part of the message you are sending to others.**

**Communication with others is composed of:**

Words you choose = 7%

Voice qualities = 38%

Physiology = 55%

Voice tone, inflection and pauses are more important than the words you choose to get your message across.

The Physiology of communication: Eye contact is vital; make sure you look in the person's left eye when you are speaking or listening. Mirroring their physiology, matching their tone, and matching the rhythm of who you are speaking with are also great methods for connecting. For example, when connecting with a typical New Yorker, that person's speed of language and intonation will be different than the speed and intonation of the typical person from the south. Don't fake an accent; just match the intonation and speed and body language of whoever you are communicating with and you will get a better connection. You have a better chance to save their life if they connect with you and these techniques will achieve that.

**Type 2. Communication with yourself: "Your psychology is affected by what you stack in your head." and "Every day stand guard at the door of your mind."**

Self talk = change your story; you change your LIFE!!! The story you tell yourself sets you up for success or failure. Words have an incredible power; you have to be aware of the power of words, then use this to your advantage. Words you say to yourself can instantly change the state you are in. Advertisers know this. For example, say you are watching a western on TV; then a Hallmark commercial with a puppy and a child are there in front of you. Your state can change instantly. Just like a Hallmark commercial can change your state at any time, you can master the ability to change your state yourself. Tony Robbins is a master at teaching how to change your state. Here are some techniques….

One technique is to be aware of your self-talk. If you refer to yourself as "I am strong, dynamic and vital," you will have a totally different state than if you refer to yourself as "I am slow and never follow through." Building your personal power will help you to master any communication. If you enter into a conversation with dynamic confidence, you will be able to lead people to health. Lives depend on your ability to communicate. Think of the choices you have to use self talk. Below are some examples of empowering self-talk and life-draining self-talk:

I am… **(Empowering = vital, confident, powerful) or (Life draining = tired, confused, sore)**

People are … **(Empowering = joyous, happy, loving) or (Life draining = selfish, manipulative, liars)**

She/he is … **(Empowering = understanding, loving, caring) or (Life draining = bitch, idiot, full of S#@&T)**


Tony Robbins has some of the greatest techniques on the planet for changing your mindset. Embody the incantations; use your body and your voice with enough intensity and repetitions so it sticks in your mind. *"Don't hope to be in a good state; DEMAND it."* This is an excerpt from a Tony Robbins YouTube exercise on self talk and the difference between incantations and affirmations. Incantations are *said aloud with full body movements* to change your state to one of empowerment. Just say the following incantation out loud with enthusiasm and full body language, and you will get goose bumps if you do it right.

*"I now command my subconscious mind to direct me to help as many people as possible today, to better their lives, by giving me the strength, the emotion, the persuasion, the brevity, the focus, whatever it takes to change their lives NOW."*

**The person who is most certain is going to influence the situation over those who are looking for certainty.**

Try this one on abundance; remember to say it out loud with full enthusiasm!!!

**Abundance:** *"God's wealth is circulating in my life and flows to me in avalanches of abundance; all of my needs, desires and goals are met instantly by infinite intelligence. For I am one with God and God is everything."* Now imagine the abundance in your life and feel grateful, and feel the feelings that the abundance gives.

Those are techniques to change your state. And that will change your mind set. This will change your certainty and allow you to lead people to health. **Chiropractors are the largest drugless health care profession on earth. You have the knowledge to change the world and now you have some techniques to save lives.**

Another point: a lot of Chiropractors have a scarcity mindset and they look to set up in areas that have few Chiropractors or a low Chiropractor-to-population ratio. Do fast food restaurants have that mindset? Heck no! Fast food restaurants are clustered together. What about car dealerships? They are always clumped together. Just keep in mind that you have *no* competition; you are *unique*. Every man, woman and child deserves to be checked for subluxations. Every man, woman and child is exposed to misinformation from the current medical authorities and *it is our responsibility and our duty to educate and save lives through marketing.*

# Study Materials:

Below is a must read; Chet Holmes has come up with "Education Based Marketing" that is vital for Chiropractic. This is mind expanding information.

http://www.chetholmes.com/media/documents/Chapter4_M YS_NEW.pdf

**Tony Robbins Seminars**:

Get to "Unleash the Power Within." This seminar is 4 days to break down barriers you may have to achieving wealth.

http://www.tonyrobbins.com/

Fill your mind with only empowering thoughts, books, videos. You must train your mind and master the principals in this book. Invest in yourself go to seminars with like minded people and groups, read books and biographies of people who have made a difference. Lives depend on it.


Now go out there and *Seize the Day*!!!

Dr John Bergman, Your Honored Colleague

For more great marketing tips scan the QR code below or go to http://0s4.com/r/YCUADN

# NOTES:

GOALS ARE JUST DREAMS...UNTIL YOU WRITE THEM
DOWN AND TAKE ACTION!

Made in the USA
Middletown, DE
13 June 2018